W9-AVR-633

How It Works

The Science of Sports The Science

Sports Illustrated KIDS

BY DAVID DREIER

Consultant:
Alan Nathan
Department of Physics
University of Illinois at
Urbana-Champaign

CAPSTONE PRESS
a capstone imprint

Sports Illustrated KIDS The Science of Sports is published by Capstone Press,
151 Good Counsel Drive, P.O. Box 669, Mankato, Minnesota 56002.
www.capstonepress.com
Copyright © 2010 by Capstone Press, a Capstone imprint. All rights reserved.
No part of this publication may be reproduced in whole or in part, or stored in a
retrieval system, or transmitted in any form or by any means, electronic, mechanical, photocopying,
recording, or otherwise, without written permission of the publisher or, where applicable, Time Inc.
For information regarding permission, write to Capstone Press,
151 Good Counsel Drive, P.O. Box 669, Dept. R, Mankato, Minnesota 56002.

Sports Illustrated Kids is a trademark of Time Inc. Used with permission.
Printed in the United States of America in Melrose Park, Illinois.

092009
005620LKS10

Books published by Capstone Press are manufactured with paper
containing at least 10 percent post-consumer waste.

Library of Congress Cataloging-in-Publication Data
Dreier, David Louis.
    Baseball : how it works / by David Dreier.
    p. cm. — (Sports Illustrated Kids. The science of sports)
    Summary: "Describes the science behind the sport of baseball, including offense, defense,
stadiums, and individual players who have mastered the sport" — Provided by publisher.
    ISBN 978-1-4296-4020-6 (library binding)
    ISBN 978-1-4296-4872-1 (paperback)
    1. Baseball — Juvenile literature. 2. Sports sciences — Juvenile literature. I. Title. II. Series.
GV867.5.D75 2010
796.357 — dc22   2009041341

Editorial Credits
Anthony Wacholtz, editor; Ted Williams, designer; Jo Miller, media researcher;
    Eric Manske, production specialist

Design Elements
Shutterstock/Eray Haciosmanoglu; kamphi

Photo Credits
AP Images, 27, 35
Capstone Studio/Karon Dubke, 36 (middle and bottom), 37 (all)
Getty Images Inc./Dilip Vishwanat, 29; Hunter Martin, 36 (top);
    Jim Rogash, 25 (bottom); Jonathan Daniel, 17, 39; Ronald Martinez, 31 (bottom);
    Transcendental Graphics/Mark Rucker, 30 (bottom), 31 (top)
Landor LLC/Kyodo, 28
Library of Congress/Keystone View Co. Inc. of N.Y., 7 (bottom)
MLB Photos via Getty Images Inc./Paul Spinelli, 10–11
Photo Researchers, Inc/Edward Kinsman, 7 (top)
Shutterstock/bdp, cover (baseball, macro shot); carroteater, 6; Dennis Ku, 22 (all), 23 (both); Paul
    Brennan, cover (home plate); R. Gino Santa Maria, 40–41; Tischenko Irina, cover (baseball), 25 (top)
Sports Illustrated/Al Tielemans, 9, 12, 14, 33, 42, 43; Bob Rosato, cover (middle and right), 32;
    Damian Strohmeyer, 1, 18, 19 (top), 26, 30 (top), 34 (bottom); David E. Klutho, cover (left);
    Heinz Kluetmeier, 16, 20; John Biever, cover (top), 3, 15 (top), 34–35 (top); John G. Zimmerman, 44;
    John W. McDonough, 4–5, 21; Peter Read Miller, 15 (bottom), 19 (bottom), 38, 45; Simon Bruty, 13, 24

TABLE OF CONTENTS

103972

No other professional sport in America has a history as rich as baseball. Major League Baseball has been thrilling sports fans for more than 100 years. People love to hear the crack of the bat and to see amazing catches from star players.

But baseball is more than just a good show. It's a science showcase. From the motion of a curveball to the force of the bat that sends a ball soaring, science is involved. The elements of the game are examples of both physics and the abilities of the human body. Let's join the crowd at "the national pastime" and see what science can tell us about what's happening on the field.

90 ft (27.4 m)

90 ft (27.4 m)

Balls occasionally clear the fence in fair territory but then curve into foul territory. Until 1930, these were not home runs. They were foul balls.

90 ft (27.4 m)

127.4 ft (38.8 m)

At the very heart of baseball is — you guessed it — the baseball! The makeup of this small, white sphere has changed very little for decades.

A major-league baseball must have:
▶ a CIRCUMFERENCE between 9 and 9.25 inches (23 and 23.5 centimeters).
▶ a weight between 5 and 5.25 ounces (142 and 149 grams).
▶ two pieces of cowhide laced together with red waxed cotton thread.
▶ lacing with exactly 108 stitches.

Baseballs made for major-league games are tested in two ways. In one test, baseballs are compressed by a powerful press. When the pressure is released, a ball must regain its shape to within .08 inch (.2 centimeter).

Another test is for "springiness," which affects how much the ball bounces. Balls are fired by an air cannon at a wood surface at 60 miles (96.5 kilometers) per hour. The speed at which each ball bounces back is measured. Major-league standards state that a ball must rebound between 51.4 and 57.8 percent of its starting VELOCITY.

CIRCUMFERENCE — a curved line that forms the outside edge of a circle
VELOCITY — a measurement of both the speed and direction an object is moving

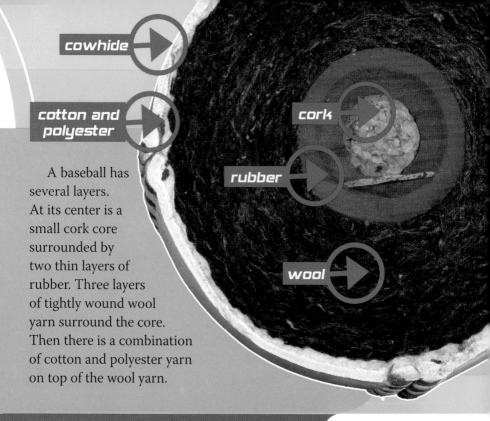

cowhide

cotton and polyester

cork

rubber

wool

A baseball has several layers. At its center is a small cork core surrounded by two thin layers of rubber. Three layers of tightly wound wool yarn surround the core. Then there is a combination of cotton and polyester yarn on top of the wool yarn.

In the late 1800s, most balls were made of rubber and hand-wound yarn. These balls were covered with horsehide and lost their shape during the game. A single ball was often used for an entire game. By the end of the game, it had become a discolored lump. It was hard to hit these balls very far, even when they were fresh out of the box. After a few innings of play, it was impossible.

Cork-centered baseballs were introduced in 1911. They were better than previous balls and could be hit farther. In the 1920s, baseballs were further improved. Machines started being used to tightly wind the yarn around the core.

Babe Ruth

Before the new balls, home runs were rare. The greatest hitter of this "Dead Ball Era" was Ty Cobb of the Detroit Tigers. He never hit more than 12 homers in a season. With the new balls, Yankee slugger Babe Ruth introduced an era of long-ball hitting. Babe Ruth hit 40 or more home runs in a season 11 times.

BASEBALL BATS

Baseball bats are another key aspect of the game. Bats differ from one another. They vary in length, weight, and material. Bats in the minor and major leagues are made of wood. Metal bats are used at the college level.

One surprising difference between bats is a concept called swing weight, or in physics terms, the moment of inertia. A bat that weighs the same as another can feel either lighter or heavier when it is swung. This swing weight is determined by the distribution of mass in the bat.

A

B   center of mass

Although both of these bats have the same weight, bat B has a higher swing weight than bat A. That is because bat B has a center of mass farther from the handle than bat A. The center of mass is the point at which the bat would balance on a knife edge, with equal weight on each side.

The bats used in the major leagues can be no more than 2.75 inches (7 centimeters) in **DIAMETER**. Their maximum length is 42 inches (107 centimeters). Most players use bats less than 36 inches (91 centimeters) long with a weight of about 32 ounces (907 grams). The range of weights is 31 to 36 ounces (879 to 1,021 grams) for most players.

DIAMETER — the length of a straight line through the center of a circle

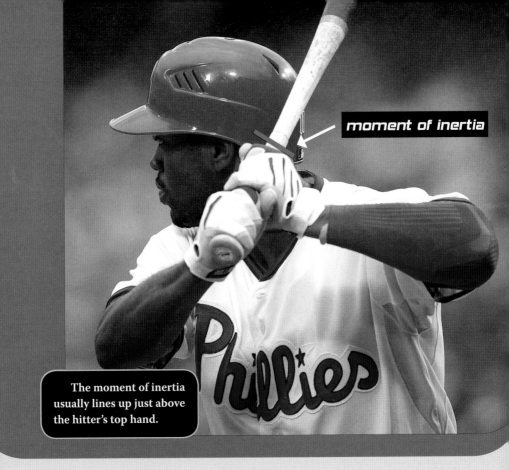

moment of inertia

The moment of inertia usually lines up just above the hitter's top hand.

A higher swing weight means a bat is harder to swing. That's because the bat has a higher moment of inertia. A bat's moment of inertia is measured from the bat's pivot point, a point 6 inches (15 centimeters) from the knob of the handle.

Choking up on the bat makes it easier to swing, since the swing weight has decreased. It also allows the batter to have better control of the bat, improving his chances of making good contact with the ball. However, choking up reduces the speed of the bat at the impact point. Therefore, the batter cannot hit a ball as hard when choking up.

CORKING A BAT

A batter can reduce the swing weight — illegally — by corking the bat. To cork a bat, a player hollows it out. He then inserts a light material, usually cork, to replace the wood. Corking makes a bat easier to swing and can help raise a player's batting average. But it won't help him hit more home runs. The faster swing won't make up for the lower mass in the barrel of the bat.

CHAPTER 2

▷ OFFENSE

Major-league baseball scouts have a phrase they use: "Good field, no hit." It means a player plays defense well but is poor at offense. Hitting a perfectly placed fastball or curveball is one of the hardest jobs in pro sports.

100 ms

75 ms

SPOTTING THE BALL
It takes about 100 milliseconds for the batter to see the ball.

CALCULATING
The batter has another 75 milliseconds in which his brain must process the visual information. This is when he estimates the speed of the pitch.

HAND-EYE COORDINATION

Hitting a pitch requires incredible eyesight and reflexes. Researchers have learned that the most successful hitters have brains that can process visual information faster than normal. These hitters can detect the spin of a ball as soon as the pitcher releases it. They claim to see the ball in what they call "slightly slower" motion.

When the pitcher fires a 90-mph fastball at the plate, the batter must react in an instant. He has less than .25 second to see the pitch, judge its speed, decide what to do, and start his swing. Then the bat has to collide with the ball within a fraction of an inch of dead center at exactly the right moment.

THE SWING

The swing takes 150 milliseconds. A batter can check his swing within 50 milliseconds, but after that he's committed. The bat is then moving too fast to be stopped — about 80 miles (129 kilometers) per hour at its peak.

25 ms   25 ms   150 ms

DECIDING

The batter has just 25 milliseconds to decide if he should swing. In another 25 milliseconds, he must decide on a swing pattern: high, low, inside, or outside.

SWINGING THE BAT

The batter must start his stride and his swing early. This usually happens when the ball is about 20 feet (6 meters) and 150 milliseconds from the plate. Then, if the batter has done everything right, the bat will make contact with the ball.

WHEN BAT MEETS BALL

When a batter slams his bat into a speeding fastball, the bat puts a huge force on the ball. The amount of force depends on the mass of the bat and the speed at which it meets the ball.

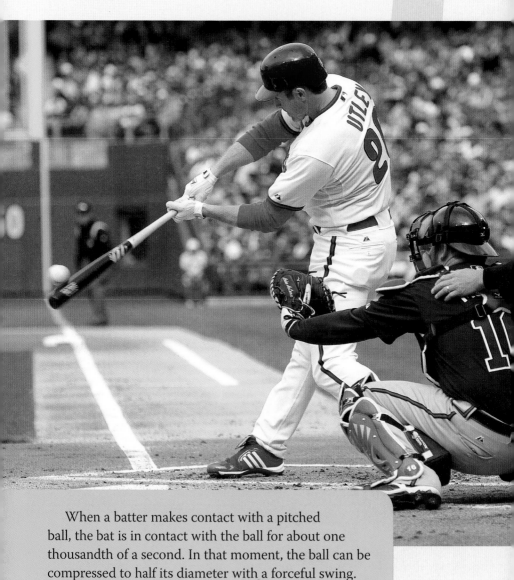

When a batter makes contact with a pitched ball, the bat is in contact with the ball for about one thousandth of a second. In that moment, the ball can be compressed to half its diameter with a forceful swing.

The amount of force applied to a ball by a bat depends on two things. They are the mass in the barrel of the bat and the sum of the pitched ball and bat speed. A big-league player can hit a 90-mph pitch with a powerful force. The force can be more than 8,000 pounds (3,629 kilograms) for the millisecond that the bat is in contact with the ball. The ball leaves the bat at a speed of about 110 mph.

Players try to choose a bat that gives them the right combination of weight and swing speed. A heavy bat will bring more mass to bear on the ball but will be harder to swing. A lighter bat will be easier to swing, but it will put less force on the ball. Most importantly, a batter needs to choose a bat with a swing weight that is right for him.

A SOLID HIT

Smacking the ball for an extra-base hit or a home run requires more than just meeting the ball at the right moment. The batter has to strike the ball with the bat's "sweet spot." The sweet spot is a region between 5 and 7 inches (13 and 18 centimeters) from the barrel end of the bat. When a player hits the ball with the sweet spot, he can feel it through his hands.

When a bat strikes a ball, the force of the collision causes the bat to vibrate. If the player hits the ball with the sweet spot of the bat, there is less vibration. Hitting the ball with the sweet spot will feel the best in the batter's hands and result in the hardest-hit ball.

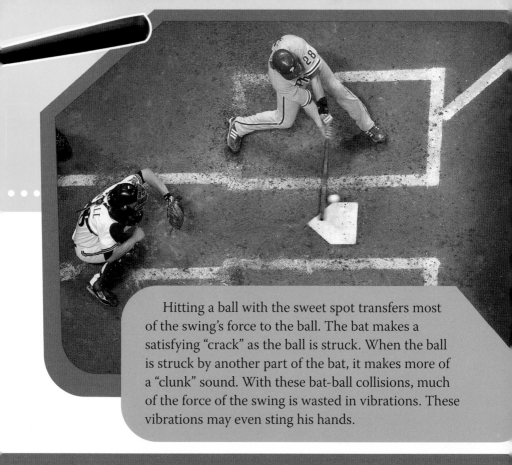

Hitting a ball with the sweet spot transfers most of the swing's force to the ball. The bat makes a satisfying "crack" as the ball is struck. When the ball is struck by another part of the bat, it makes more of a "clunk" sound. With these bat-ball collisions, much of the force of the swing is wasted in vibrations. These vibrations may even sting his hands.

SCIENCE OF THE BUNT

The opposite of a long drive is a bunt. The bunt is often used to advance a player on base. To bunt, the batter holds the bat at both ends and places it horizontally in front of the pitch. As the ball hits the bat, the player pulls the bat back in the direction of the pitch to absorb the ball's **MOMENTUM**. The ball should hit the bottom half of the bat so the ball angles toward the ground. If the ball hits the top half of the bat, it will pop up. If a bunt is done properly, the ball loses most of its energy in the collision. It bounces off the bat toward the ground and rolls slowly away.

MOMENTUM — a property of a moving object equal to its mass times its velocity

WHEN A PITCH GOES WILD

Sometimes a pitcher doesn't put the ball where he wants it. A batter who gets hit by a pitched ball has a free pass to first base. But a pitch to an unprotected part of the body can also send a player to the hospital. Batting helmets can protect players from severe head injuries.

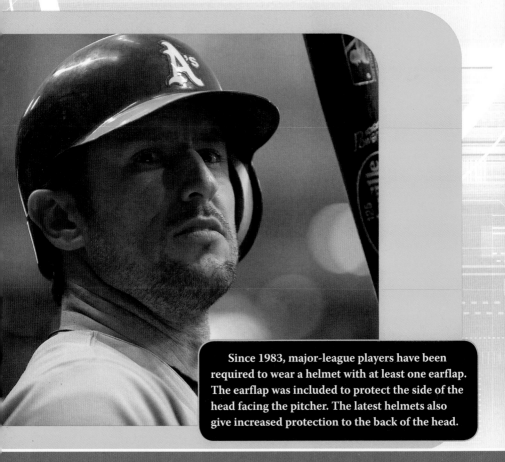

Since 1983, major-league players have been required to wear a helmet with at least one earflap. The earflap was included to protect the side of the head facing the pitcher. The latest helmets also give increased protection to the back of the head.

DEATH AT THE PLATE

The only major-league player ever killed by a pitched ball was Ray Chapman of the Cleveland Indians. On Aug. 16, 1920, Chapman was hit in the head by a ball thrown by Yankee pitcher Carl Mays. Chapman was taken to a hospital, where he died. It would be 50 years before batting helmets were required in the big leagues.

A player could suffer a severe brain injury if struck in the head by a pitch. The ball could push the side of the skull inward and possibly break it. The brain would slam against the other side of the skull. Shock waves from the impact would go through the brain. Fortunately, the helmet absorbs most of the ball's force. The player may get jarred by the impact, but he is usually protected from a serious head injury.

RUNNING THE BASES

Unless you sock a home run, scoring in baseball usually requires some fast running from one base to another. There are two ways to advance on the base paths: in a straight line or in a curve. There are solid reasons for each type of running.

The shortest distance around the bases is a straight path from one base to the next. That's fine for a one-base advance. But if a player is going for extra bases, running in straight lines is not a good strategy. The player could not run at full speed to a base, because his momentum would carry him past the base. To prevent that, he would have to slow down as he approached each base and then stop and turn toward the next base. He could then pick up speed again. If the player rounds the base, he won't have to slow down as much when he reaches it.

momentum = mass x velocity

GOING FOR THE STEAL

One way to advance on the bases is to steal a base. The base most commonly stolen is second. By moving from first base to second, a runner puts himself in position to score if a teammate hits a single.

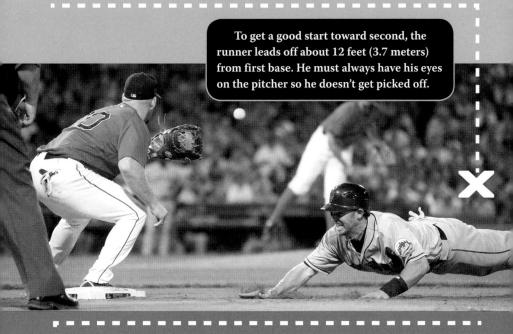

To get a good start toward second, the runner leads off about 12 feet (3.7 meters) from first base. He must always have his eyes on the pitcher so he doesn't get picked off.

As soon as the pitcher begins his delivery toward home plate, the runner makes his move. It takes a good runner about 3.3 seconds to cover the remaining 78 feet (23.8 meters) to second base.

The runner tries to reach second base before the ball gets there. While he runs, the catcher must receive the pitch and throw the ball to second base. The player covering second must catch the ball and make the tag. How much time do these actions take on average? About 3.3 seconds. It's no wonder baseball is called "a game of inches!"

INTO THE DIRT!

When a player runs at top speed to a base to beat a throw, he almost always slides. Good sliding can be as important as fast running.

One reason for sliding is to come in under the ball being thrown to the base. This action can provide the runner an extra moment if the throw is high. The baseman has to catch the ball and then reach down for the tag. Catchers try to make tagging easier for the baseman by throwing the ball so it arrives close to the base.

The other reason for sliding is to reduce forward momentum. A player running at top speed has to slow down when he gets close to the base or he'll go right past it. Sliding is equivalent to applying the brakes in a car. By throwing himself into the dirt a few feet from the base, the runner uses **FRICTION** to reduce his forward speed. He goes from full speed to a full stop in a fraction of a second.

FRICTION — the force created by a moving object as it rubs against a surface

Baseball players and fans have debated the best way to slide into the bases. Many players have said that sliding headfirst feels a bit faster. In 2008, Dr. David A. Peters studied the difference between the two slides. He found that a headfirst slide is indeed faster than a feetfirst slide.

Peters explained that the difference has to do with the body's **CENTER OF GRAVITY**. The center of gravity varies between people, but it is somewhere in the lower abdomen. The position of a runner's center of gravity during the slide determines how fast the player slides into a base. During a headfirst slide, a runner's arms are outstretched toward the base. The runner's fingertips are far from his center of gravity, so they reach the base more quickly. The player reaches the base more slowly during a feetfirst slide because his feet are closer to his center of gravity.

CENTER OF GRAVITY — the point around which an object's weight is evenly distributed

▷ DEFENSE

CHAPTER 3

The pitcher has to use all of his skill to confuse batters. The most basic pitch he can throw is the fastball. If a pitcher can't put real "heat" on his fastball, he isn't likely to last long.

A pitcher goes through six basic steps when making a pitch. These phases are designed to generate **TORQUE** in the pitcher's body. That force is then transferred to the ball.

THE FASTBALL

WINDUP:
The pitcher begins his motion. He raises his hands together, turns to the side, and lifts his knee.

STRIDE:
The pitcher's arms separate as he moves his leading leg toward home plate.

ARM COCK:
As his leading foot touches the ground, the pitcher cocks his throwing arm behind his head.

22   **TORQUE** — a force that causes rotation

THE PITCHING "SPEED LIMIT"

Olympic runners and swimmers constantly set new record times. In baseball, on the other hand, the record for the fastest pitch is almost impossible to break. In the early 1900s, pitchers like Walter Johnson of the Washington Senators threw fastballs up to 100 mph. Despite advances in training, few pitchers today can top 100 mph. No one can throw a ball much faster than that. Why?

Dr. Glenn Fleisig, a biomechanics engineer, says there is a reason. He explains that pitching a 100-mph fastball puts a lot of stress on a pitcher's arm. Throwing a ball much more than 100 mph would create too much torque in a pitcher's arm. This could cause tendons and ligaments in the arm to snap.

To prove his point, Fleisig conducted tests with the arms of corpses. The elbows of the corpses went through increasing amounts of rotational force. At a torque of about 80 newton-meters, a ligament in the arm snapped. That is about the amount of torque required to throw a fastball 100 mph. A pitcher who applies much more force than that won't get a faster pitch — he'll get a badly damaged arm!

ARM ACCELERATION:

The pitcher whips his arm around, forward, and down, releasing the ball toward the plate. The force of his arm movement produces forward momentum on the ball.

ARM DECELERATION:

Having released the ball, the pitcher brings his leg down. His arm follows the path across his body and comes to a stop.

THROWING THEM A CURVE

Dizzy Dean, a star pitcher for the St. Louis Cardinals in the 1930s, loved to hurl fastballs. "I liked to just rear back and fog 'em in," he said after he retired. But even the best fastball pitchers can't depend on that one pitch. A pitcher has to keep batters guessing what the next pitch will be.

One way to fool the batter is with "breaking balls." These pitches curve or drop in various ways because of the spin put on them. Breaking pitches include the screwball and the slider. But the most common breaking pitch is the curveball.

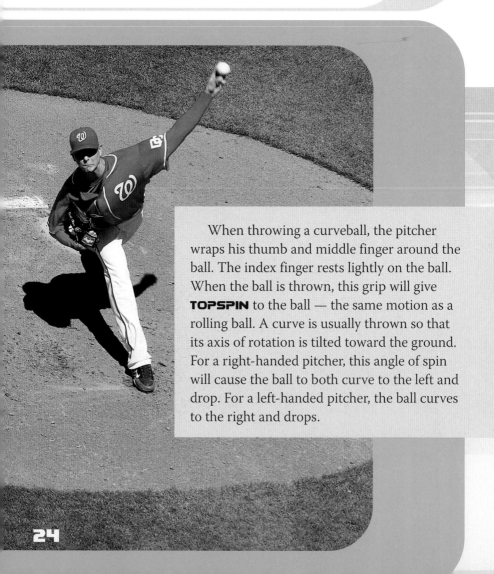

When throwing a curveball, the pitcher wraps his thumb and middle finger around the ball. The index finger rests lightly on the ball. When the ball is thrown, this grip will give **TOPSPIN** to the ball — the same motion as a rolling ball. A curve is usually thrown so that its axis of rotation is tilted toward the ground. For a right-handed pitcher, this angle of spin will cause the ball to both curve to the left and drop. For a left-handed pitcher, the ball curves to the right and drops.

The motion of a curveball is caused by the Magnus effect. When a spinning baseball flies toward the plate, the spin creates two different layers of pressure. There is a high-pressure layer of air on the side of the ball that spins in the direction of the ball's motion. There is a low-pressure layer on the other side. The high-pressure air produces a force toward the area of lower pressure. With a curveball, this creates a curving motion away from a straight line of flight.

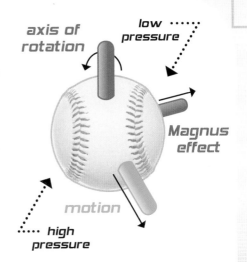

axis of
rotation

low
pressure

Magnus
effect

motion

high
pressure

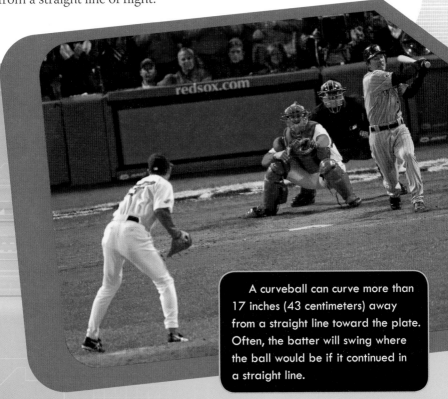

A curveball can curve more than 17 inches (43 centimeters) away from a straight line toward the plate. Often, the batter will swing where the ball would be if it continued in a straight line.

TOPSPIN — spin that is in the same direction as that of a rolling ball

THE PITCH THAT FOOLS EVERYONE

Perhaps the hardest pitch to hit is the knuckleball. This pitch, which is thrown with very little spin, is completely unpredictable. And it's just as hard to catch as it is to hit. Los Angeles Dodgers manager Joe Torre, a former catcher, said, "You don't catch the knuckleball, you defend against it." Another former catcher, Bob Uecker, remarked that the way to catch a knuckleball is to "wait till it stops rolling, then go to the backstop and pick it up."

A well-thrown knuckleball is said to "flutter" or "dance" on its way to the plate. It moves to one side and then to the other. It's difficult for the batter to know where the ball will be when it arrives at the plate.

HOYT AND THE GIANT MITT

One of the best knuckleball pitchers of all time was Hoyt Wilhelm. He pitched for several teams from the 1950s to the 1970s. While with the Baltimore Orioles, he kept catchers on their toes with his knuckleballs. In 1960, Orioles manager Paul Richards created a huge mitt for his catchers. The mitt had a circumference of 45 inches (114 centimeters). But other teams objected. In 1965, Major League Baseball officials made a rule about the catcher's mitt. The circumference of the glove couldn't be more than 38 inches (97 centimeters).

Hall of Fame catcher Ray Schalk displays the famous large mitt created by Paul Richards.

The knuckleball was originally thrown by holding the ball with the knuckles. Today, though, most knuckleball pitchers grip the ball with their fingertips. The goal is to throw the ball with almost no rotation.

A knuckleball's movement is caused by the raised seams of the ball. The seams of a baseball affect the air currents as the ball moves through the air. If a knuckleball had absolutely no rotation, it wouldn't do much. A knuckleball pitcher tries to throw the ball so that it rotates very, very slowly. The ball should make no more than one full turn on its way to the plate. With this slow rotation, the seams of the ball change position just enough for the ball to move unpredictably on its way to the plate.

A RISKY JOB

No one in baseball is as prone to injuries as the pitcher. A pitcher's arm goes through the same motions and forces over and over again. These motions can damage tendons and ligaments. As a result, a pitcher can develop several problems in his elbow and shoulder. Sometimes, these injuries can end a pitcher's career.

Some pitchers develop a condition called "pitcher's elbow." Ligaments in the elbow become inflamed and may develop small tears. The pitcher experiences pain and swelling that start at the elbow and may travel down the forearm. The condition can usually be treated with rest and medicine. Sometimes, though, the pitcher has to have surgery on his elbow.

Pitchers can also have problems with a **ROTATOR CUFF**. These conditions include tendonitis and bursitis. Tendonitis is caused when tendons in the pitching arm become inflamed. Bursitis is a condition in which the bursas — fluid-filled sacs that provide cushion between tendons and bones — become inflamed. Rest and mild exercise will usually cause these conditions to fade.

ROTATOR CUFF — a group of muscles and tendons in the shoulder

The worst shoulder injury is called a labrum tear. The labrum is a layer of cartilage between the humerus, or the upper arm bone, and the socket in the shoulder. With the ligaments, the labrum keeps the end of the humerus in place. A torn labrum usually requires surgery. Unfortunately, the operation is rarely completely successful, at least for pitchers. Very few pitchers with a torn labrum can have a successful career after surgery.

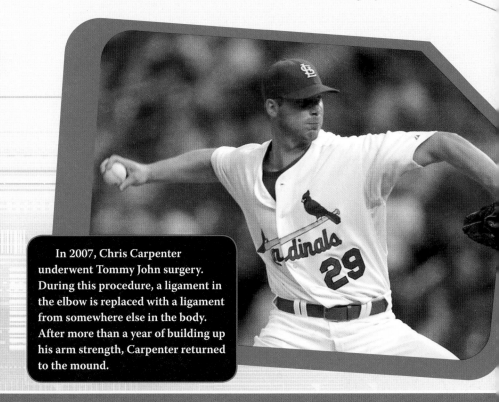

In 2007, Chris Carpenter underwent Tommy John surgery. During this procedure, a ligament in the elbow is replaced with a ligament from somewhere else in the body. After more than a year of building up his arm strength, Carpenter returned to the mound.

HURT ON THE MOUND

Pitchers also have to worry about their position on the field. The pitcher's mound is only 60 feet (18.3 meters) from the batter. A pitcher is usually slightly off-balance when the batter swings. He may not be able to dodge a line drive coming at him at 110 miles (177 kilometers) per hour.

One of the first serious injuries to a pitcher happened in 1922. Pitcher Bill Hubbell of the Philadelphia Phillies was hit in the head by a line drive. People feared Hubble might die from the injury. He not only survived — he pitched for three more years!

Another terrible accident occurred on May 7, 1957. Herb Score, a young pitcher from the Cleveland Indians, had a line drive smash into his right eye. He was carried from the field with blood pouring from his eye, nose, and mouth. Although he pitched the next year, he was still shaken up by the injury. He was traded to the White Sox in 1959, and he retired after the 1962 season.

A FIELDER'S FRIEND

The most basic piece of equipment for defensive play is the glove or mitt. Gloves have evolved more than any other piece of baseball equipment. They have two purposes: to protect a player's hands and to make it easier for him to catch a thrown or batted ball.

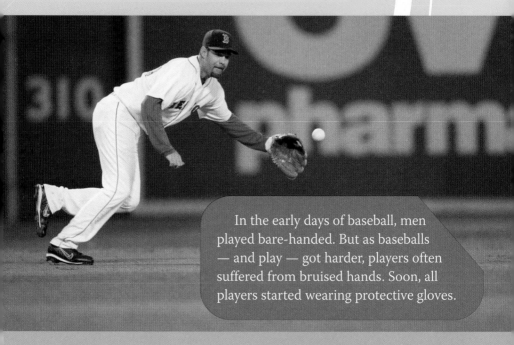

In the early days of baseball, men played bare-handed. But as baseballs — and play — got harder, players often suffered from bruised hands. Soon, all players started wearing protective gloves.

▶ THE FIRST GLOVES

The very first gloves, used in the 1870s, were just a leather covering. Because they had no fingers, they provided only a little cushioning against hard throws. They absorbed a small amount of force from the incoming ball.

▶ COMPLETE FINGERS

By the end of the 1800s, players were using "workman's gloves." These provided better protection for the players' hands. However, they were not much bigger than a player's hand. Their small size still made it difficult to catch balls.

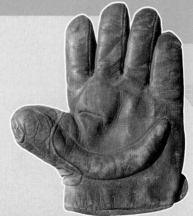

▶ GLOVES GET WEBBING

Webbing was a part of baseball gloves by the 1920s. Webbing allowed players to catch a ball between their thumb and index finger. With this design, almost none of the ball's force was transferred to the player's hand.

▶ CONNECTING THE FINGERS

By the late 1940s, the fingers of gloves were laced together to give the fielder greater control over the glove. The gloves and the webbing had also gotten bigger. These changes allowed the glove to absorb even more of the ball's force.

▶ A MODERN GLOVE

Gloves have become more useful for fielders over the years. In addition to protecting the player's palm from injury, today's gloves have even larger webbing and a hinged structure. The hinged web makes it easier for a player to snap the glove closed around the ball.

Until the 1940s, baseball players often left their gloves on the field. When it was time for their side to bat, they simply dropped their gloves near their position. When the players returned to the field, they picked up their gloves again and put them on. Gloves lying on the field were considered a normal part of the game, like bases. A ball

PLAYING THE INFIELD

Infielders must be able to scoop up fast-moving ground balls and catch blazing line drives. They must also be able to make accurate throws to bases to beat the runners. It takes a lot of practice to be a good infielder.

Unless a ground ball is hit really hard — when it may be necessary to dive for it — an infielder must charge the ball. Charging gets him to the ball faster. In this way, he may be able to reduce the distance that he has to throw out the runner. A shorter throwing distance means a shorter throwing time. If the infielder can position himself in front of the ball, he straddles the spot. He is making himself into a wall. If the ball takes a bad hop, it is likely to hit the infielder's chest or one of his legs.

PICKING UP SPEED?

Many ballplayers claim that batted balls sometimes speed up when they hit the ground. Physicists say that a batted ball can speed up when it hits the ground. But this is only if the spinning velocity from the topspin is greater than the ball's forward velocity. However, it is very unlikely that a batter could hit the ball with enough topspin to make this happen. A batted ball with a lot of topspin loses less forward speed when it hits the ground than an ordinary grounder. The infielder sees this difference as an increase in the ball's speed.

A line drive comes off the bat at a speed up to 110 miles (177 kilometers) per hour. An infielder wants to catch a speeding line drive with minimal sting to his hands. To do so, he is likely to bring his glove and other hand in toward his body as he traps the ball in the glove. This backward movement prolongs the time in which the ball goes from full velocity to zero velocity. The longer that time can be extended, the less force will be put on the glove from the ball.

THE SOUND OF A HIT

An outfielder usually can't wait to see where a fly ball is heading. The longer he takes to make his move, the less time he'll have to get into the right spot to catch the ball. Instead, outfielders learn to judge where the hit is going. They listen to the sound made by the bat hitting the ball. If an outfielder uses his eyes alone, it takes him about 1.5 seconds to figure out the arc of a fly ball. That time can mean the difference between catching the ball and missing it.

The sound of the bat hitting the ball reaches outfielders in about three-tenths of a second. If a batter hits the ball solidly, the bat makes a sharp "crack." That sound is produced by air exploding out from between the bat and the ball. When an outfielder hears the "crack," he starts running backward, knowing the ball has been well hit. When a ball is poorly hit, the bat vibrates and produces a "clunk." If an outfielder hears that sound, he starts running forward.

A LEGENDARY CATCH

Sometimes outfielders make catches that defy belief. Such a catch was made by New York Giants center fielder Willie Mays in the 1954 World Series against the Cleveland Indians. In the eighth inning of Game 1 at New York's Polo Grounds, Vic Wertz of the Indians came to plate. The score was tied 2-2 with two men on base. Wertz hit an incredible blast toward the center-field wall, 483 feet (147 meters) from home plate. Mays turned and ran toward the wall. As he neared it, he put up his glove and caught the ball over his shoulder. It was one of the most amazing catches ever made. The Giants went on to win both the game and the World Series.

THE CROW HOP

Just as a pitcher uses a windup to add force to a pitch, an outfielder must add extra "oomph" to make a long throw. A throwing technique often used by outfielders is called the crow hop. It adds both power and accuracy to a long throw.

1

The player brings his arms to his chest and makes a step forward onto the foot opposite his throwing arm.

2

The fielder then makes a slight hop to transfer his weight onto his back leg.

WORTH THE EXTRA STEP?

Some coaches are not enthusiastic about the crow hop. They say it takes too long. As one coach explains it, using the crow hop may enable an outfielder to throw a ball at a speed of 90 miles (145 kilometers) per hour and reach home plate. However, it takes a fielder about 1.5 seconds to make the crow hop and release the ball. It might be better if he were to just pick up the ball and fire it to an infielder. He wouldn't get as much speed on the ball, but he would be saving up to a full second of time in making the throw.

3

The fielder leans back on his trailing leg and brings his throwing arm down alongside that leg. At the same time, he raises his front leg, which is bent at the knee.

4

The player brings his body forward, transferring his weight back onto his front leg, to generate throwing force. At the same time, he starts to bring his arm around.

5

Using all the force he has generated, the player brings his arm around and hurls the ball toward the infield.

THE MAN BEHIND THE MASK

The catcher has one of the toughest jobs in baseball. He must crouch behind the batter and catch pitches while not getting distracted by the bat. He gets hit by foul tips. He is rammed by runners trying to score a run. On top of that, his knees take a beating from all that crouching.

A catcher has to be well protected. He uses various equipment to keep from getting injured.

FACE MASK
The catcher's mask allows him to see clearly while protecting his face from missed pitches and foul tips.

CHEST PROTECTOR
The chest protector covers the catcher's upper body and abdomen. It is filled with a foam or gel that absorbs impact.

CATCHER'S MITT
The mitt used by a catcher is well padded to protect his hand from blazing fastballs. Even with the extra padding, catchers often develop circulatory problems in their hand from catching so many forceful pitches.

SHIN GUARDS
These plastic coverings protect the catcher's lower legs. They feature knee pads that allow the catcher to kneel in comfort.

Because of their crouching position, catchers often suffer a torn meniscus. Menisci are a pair of C-shaped disks of cartilage in the knee joint that act as shock absorbers. When a meniscus injury occurs, the knee becomes painful when flexed. A torn meniscus can usually be repaired with surgery. Still, bad knees often shorten catchers' careers.

TRICKY POP-UPS

Catching high pop-ups is one of a catcher's hardest jobs. A pop-up can go as high as 120 feet (37 meters) and follow a weird path. The ball can follow a looping course on its way back down to the ground, crossing over its upward path. This motion is caused by the rapidly spinning force of the Magnus effect. A pop-up comes off the top of the bat, which gives it a huge amount of backspin. The Magnus force generated by the backspin causes the ball to reverse direction on the way back to the ground. Catchers chase down foul balls wherever they go — even by falling into the stands or a dugout!

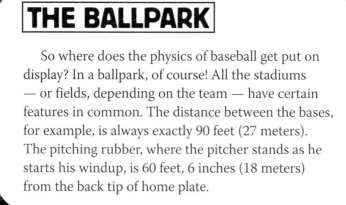

CHAPTER 4

THE BALLPARK

So where does the physics of baseball get put on display? In a ballpark, of course! All the stadiums — or fields, depending on the team — have certain features in common. The distance between the bases, for example, is always exactly 90 feet (27 meters). The pitching rubber, where the pitcher stands as he starts his windup, is 60 feet, 6 inches (18 meters) from the back tip of home plate.

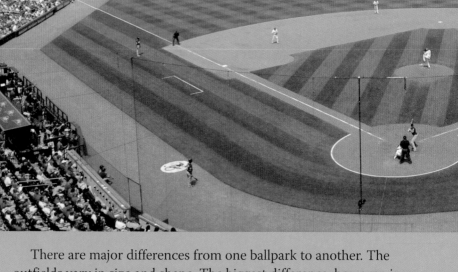

There are major differences from one ballpark to another. The outfields vary in size and shape. The biggest difference, however, is between open and enclosed stadiums. Six major-league stadiums are either fully enclosed domes or have retractable roofs. The absence of weather conditions in a park, especially wind, can greatly affect the game.

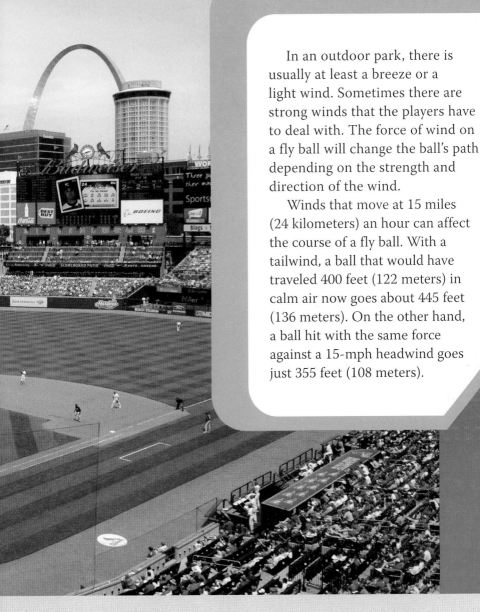

In an outdoor park, there is usually at least a breeze or a light wind. Sometimes there are strong winds that the players have to deal with. The force of wind on a fly ball will change the ball's path depending on the strength and direction of the wind.

Winds that move at 15 miles (24 kilometers) an hour can affect the course of a fly ball. With a tailwind, a ball that would have traveled 400 feet (122 meters) in calm air now goes about 445 feet (136 meters). On the other hand, a ball hit with the same force against a 15-mph headwind goes just 355 feet (108 meters).

Winds can blow in several directions in outdoor ballparks. A wind blowing straight toward the outfield will increase the chance that a fly ball will be a home run. The opposite is also true. A wind blowing toward the infield will create more air resistance and prevent some hard-hit balls from making it across the outfield wall.

THE PLAYING SURFACE

Baseball has been played on both grass and artificial turf. The two kinds of surfaces affect the game. The main difference is in the movement of ground balls.

Grounders move faster on artificial turf — which is made of plastic — than on grass. Many grounders that would be stopped by infielders on a grass field can make it past them on artificial turf. The grass field creates more friction on the ball than artificial turf does. Friction slows down the ball.

THE RISE AND FALL OF ARTIFICIAL TURF

Until 1966, all Major League Baseball games were played on grass fields. That changed with the introduction of Astroturf at the Astrodome in Houston, Texas. When the enclosed Astrodome opened in 1965, it had a grass playing field. But that didn't last long. Players in afternoon practices were blinded by sunlight coming in through panels in the dome. The owner tried to solve the problem by painting the outer surface of the dome off-white. Without sunlight, though, the grass died.

For the 1966 season, the owner of the Astrodome replaced the grass with artificial turf. The artificial grass, named AstroTurf, was basically a green plastic rug. In the following years, a number of other ballparks — even outdoor parks — replaced natural grass with artificial turf. There were several reasons for the switch, including easier maintenance and better water drainage. Some newer materials, such as FieldTurf, were more like real grass.

Nonetheless, the tide began to turn against artificial turf in the mid-1970s. People wanted baseball to once again be a game played on grass. As of 2010, only two ballparks still had artificial turf.

Infielders playing on artificial turf tend to play farther away from home plate. This gives them more range and reaction time. Then they have a better chance to get to grounders that they might otherwise not be able to reach. Balls that make it past the infielders often become doubles or triples.

In baseball, as in all sports, some players have mastered the science of their sport. Here are a few records that have been set by players with amazing abilities.

▶ LONGEST HOME RUN

Guinness World Records says the longest home run was hit by Mickey Mantle on September 10, 1960. The home run supposedly flew 634 feet (193 meters). However, most baseball experts say it is impossible to hit a baseball that distance.

Mantle still probably holds the record for the longest home run. On April 17, 1953, Mantle socked a towering homer that was thought to have traveled 565 feet (172 meters). But that distance was measured from where the ball landed after it stopped rolling, not how far it flew in the air. The actual distance was probably closer to 510 feet (155 meters). That distance was still probably far enough for it to be the longest homer ever hit in the major leagues.

▶ FASTEST TIME AROUND THE BASES

There seems to be no dispute about this one. Baseball experts agree that Evar Swanson, a leftfielder for the Cincinnati Reds, holds the title. It happened during a baserunning exhibition between games of a double header on September 15, 1929. Swanson ran the bases in 13.3 seconds. That record has held for more than 80 years.

▶ FASTEST PITCH

Guinness credits Nolan Ryan with throwing the fastest pitch in a major-league game. It says Ryan threw a fastball that flew 100.9 mph in a game on August 20, 1974. The fastest pitch ever recorded in spring training was thrown by Mark Wohlers in 1995. Wohlers threw a fastball that was clocked at 103 mph.

The fastest ball thrown anywhere might have been by Cleveland Indian pitcher Bob Feller. In 1946, Feller threw a fastball in a pitching display at Griffith Field that was clocked at 107.9 mph. That speed has been accepted by the National Baseball Hall of Fame.

▶ LONGEST THROW

Glen Gorbous holds the record for the longest throw by a pro baseball player. Gorbous played briefly as a major-league outfielder in the 1950s. After being sent to the minors, Gorbous took part in a baseball-throwing exhibition in 1957. With a running start, he threw the ball 445 feet, 10 inches (136 meters).

MEASURING HOME RUNS

In the past, the only way to measure the distance of a home run was to break out the tape measure. In recent years, home runs have been measured using special cameras and computer programs. These devices are used to calculate the arcs of home runs that leave the park. They also determine how far a long drive would have gone if it hadn't hit a scoreboard or other object. A Web site called HitTracker makes similar calculations. It even features measurements of legendary homers, such as a blast that Mickey Mantle hit against the Kansas City A's on May 22, 1963. HitTracker measured that home run at 507 feet (155 meters).

GLOSSARY

backspin (BAK-spin) — spin that is opposite in direction to that of a rolling ball

center of gravity (SEN-tur UHV GRAV-uh-tee) — the point around which an object's weight is evenly distributed

circumference (suhr-KUHM-fuhr-uhnss) — a curved line that forms the outside edge of a circle

diameter (dy-A-muh-tuhr) — the length of a straight line through the center of a circle

friction (FRIK-shuhn) — the force created by a moving object as it rubs against a surface

inertia (in-UR-shuh) — an object's state in which the object stays at rest or keeps moving in the same direction until a force acts on it

Magnus effect (MAG-nuss uh-FEKT) — a force put on a baseball or other rapidly spinning object that acts perpendicular to the axis of rotation

momentum (moh-MEN-tuhm) — a property of a moving object equal to its mass times its velocity

rotator cuff (ROH-tay-tuhr CUFF) — a group of muscles and tendons in the shoulder

topspin (TOP-spin) — spin that is in the same direction as that of a rolling ball

torque (TORK) — a force that causes rotation

velocity (vuh-LOSS-uh-tee) — a measurement of both the speed and direction an object is moving

Bow, James. *Baseball Science.* Sports Science. New York: Crabtree Publishing, 2009.

Jacobs, Greg. *The Everything Kids' Baseball Book: Today's Superstars, Great Teams, Legends, and Tips on Playing Like a Pro.* Everything Series. Avon, Mass.: Adams Media, 2006.

Levine, Shar, and Leslie Johnstone. *Sports Science.* New York: Sterling, 2006.

Solway, Andrew. *Sports Science.* Why Science Matters. Chicago: Heinemann, 2009.

INTERNET SITES

FactHound offers a safe, fun way to find Internet sites related to this book. All of the sites on Facthound have been researched by our staff.

Here's all you do:

Visit *www.facthound.com*

FactHound will fetch the best sites for you!

INDEX

EAST SMITHFIELD PUBLIC LIBRARY

3 2895 00113 3532